Camping at School

Written by Sally Odgers

Illustrated by Naomi Lewis

It had been raining every day and every night for a week. Megan looked outside one morning and saw that the river was overflowing.

"Dad! Look!" she called.
"There's water everywhere!"

Dad was worried. He turned on the radio. The first thing they heard was a flood warning for their area. "It's an emergency," said Dad. "We have to evacuate."

"What does that mean?" asked Megan.

"It means we have to leave our house and go somewhere safe," answered Dad.

Dad and Megan packed some clothes and their sleeping bags. They rolled up rugs, lifted chairs onto tables, and put books on high shelves.

"Where are we going?" asked Megan,
as they loaded the car.

"The radio said to go to the school,"
answered Dad. "It's on a hill,
so it'll be safe if there's a flood."

Dad drove slowly and carefully. He could hardly see through the pouring rain.

Megan was amazed that there could be so much rain. She thought of all the water near their house. "Will our house be okay?" she asked.

"I hope so," answered Dad.

When Dad and Megan finally arrived at the school, a lot of people were already there. It was very noisy and it smelled like wet clothes.

"Look at all these people," said Megan.

"And more will be coming," said Dad.
"Let's see how we can help."

They went into the kitchen. Some people were making soup. Others were making sandwiches. Everyone was busy. It was like a big school camp, especially when Megan saw her teacher, Mrs. Hill.

The school principal, Mr. Cunningham, came up to talk to Dad.

"Mr. Cunningham has asked me to join a rescue team," Dad told Megan. "A family is trapped by the flood. You can help Mrs. Hill while I'm gone."

Megan didn't want her dad to go.
But she thought about the family
that needed to get to a safe place.
"You go, Dad," she said. "I'll be fine."

While her dad was away, Megan helped Mrs. Hill. She helped serve soup, and she looked after the small children.

Soon it was night. Megan was very tired, but she couldn't sleep. She sat on her sleeping bag and waited for her dad.

It was late when Dad finally came back.

"Is the family all right?" asked Megan.

"Yes, they're safe now," answered Dad.
"Mrs. Hill says you were a big help here."

Megan told her dad how she had read stories to the children and played games with them. Then she took him to the kitchen, where she had saved him some soup.

Dad gave her a hug and told her she'd really helped in the emergency. Then Megan crawled into her sleeping bag and went to sleep.

When Megan woke up the next
morning, the rain had stopped.
It was safe for everyone to go home.

Megan was very happy to see that their house was safe and sound. "There was one thing I liked about all that rain," she said.

"What was that?" asked Dad.

"I liked camping at school," said Megan. "But I hope we never have to do it again!"